CORNER✳STO...

VOLUME II

BITS OF WISDOM

AND HUMOR FROM

THE PAGES OF

Progressive Farmer®

Progressive Farmer, Inc.
BIRMINGHAM, ALABAMA 35209

Foreword

I N SOME WAYS, it is reassuring that people who came before us faced many of the same challenges that we face today. And from them and their words, we can learn. We can understand and, with their help, we can meet our challenges.

This is what *Cornerstones II* is all about. We have gleaned words, both humorous and serious, about issues we all face. Useful sayings on subjects such as courage, failure, tolerance, loneliness, and persistence can be found in *Cornerstones II*. As with our first *Cornerstones*, this second book was also taken from the pages of *Progressive Farmer* magazine. So, welcome to *Cornerstones II*. Sit back, relax, and let *Cornerstones II* and our ancestors help you deal with the everyday trials of living.

—JACK ODLE

© 1992 by Progressive Farmer, Inc.
Manufactured in the United States of America

Library of Congress Catalog Card Number: 92-061662
International Standard Book Number: 0-8487-1224-2

Contents

Gratitude   4

Harvest   6

Wealth   8

Persistence   10

Enthusiasm   12

Taxes   14

Curiosity   16

Experience   18

Family   20

Democracy   22

Courage   24

Excellence   26

Indecision   28

Failure   30

Truth   32

Reading   34

Statistics   36

Humor   38

Superstition   40

Quality   42

Work   44

Loneliness   46

Art   48

Morality   50

Technology   52

Silence   54

Tolerance   56

Generosity   58

Imagination   60

Planning   62

Gratitude

In Italy, it's grazie. *In France,* merci; *and in Mexico,* gracias. *In the former Soviet Union, people say* spasibo *and in Japan,* arigato. *They say* danke *in Germany,* obrigato *in Brazil, and* hsieh hsieh *in China. No matter where you travel in the world, the meaning is the same. Only the way we say thank you is different.*

• Gratitude is the most exquisite form of courtesy.

JACQUES MARITAIN

• While I would fain have some tincture of all the virtues, there is no quality I would rather have, and be thought to have, than gratitude. For it is not only the greatest virtue, but even the mother of all the rest.

CICERO

• Gratefulness is the poor man's payment.

ENGLISH PROVERB

• He who receives a benefit should never forget it; he who bestows one would never remember it.

PIERRE CHARRON

• Let not the blessing of the plain man have little value in your eyes.

BABYLONIAN TALMUD

• Men are slower to recognize blessings than evils.

LIVY

• We seldom find people ungrateful so long as we are in a position to be beneficial.

FRANÇOIS, DUC DE ROCHEFOUCAULD

• Blow, blow, thou winter wind;
Thou are not so unkind
   as man's ingratitude.

WILLIAM SHAKESPEARE

• When you call a man ungrateful, you have no words of abuse left.

PUBLILIUS SYRUS

• If you pick up a starving dog and make him prosperous, he will not bite you. This is the principal difference between a dog and a man.

MARK TWAIN

• Gratitude is a burden upon one's imperfect nature.

LORD CHESTERFIELD

• My Dame fed her hens with mere thanks, and they laid no Eggs.

THOMAS FULLER

• Be thankful for what you have not . . . ; 'tis the only safe rule.

FINDLEY PETER DUNNE

• One good thing about having [only] one suit of clothes—you've always got your pencil.

KIN HUBBARD

• The good should be grateful to the bad—for providing the world with a basis for comparison.

SVEN HALLA

• Gratitude is one of the least articulate of the emotions, especially when it is deep.

FELIX FRANKFURTER

• Should not the giver be thankful that the receiver received? Is not giving a need? Is not receiving, mercy?

FRIEDRICH NIETZSCHE

• We mortals realize the value of our blessings only when we have lost them.

PLAUTUS

• No duty is more urgent than that of returning thanks.

ST. AMBROSE

• Who gives not thanks to men, gives not thanks to God.

JOHN LEWIS BURCKHARDT

• Gratitude is the memory of the heart.

JEAN BAPTIST MASSIEU

• You will be enriched in every way for great generosity . . . ; for the rendering of this service not only supplies the wants of the saints but also overflows in many thanksgivings to God.

II CORINTHIANS 9: 11-12

• What comes from the heart goes to the heart.

SAMUEL TAYLOR COLERIDGE

• God waits to win back his own flowers as gifts from man's hands.

RABINDRANATH TAGORE

CORNERSTONES

Harvest

Harvest is a magical time. Lunch and supper in the field, working at night by the lights of the combine and trucks; rushing to beat the rain; breakdowns, mud, dust. Drained by long hours, you become ruled by your emotions. Anxiety, anger, joy, relief, they all surface. Few times in life make us feel as alive as harvest time.

• It was Autumn, and incessant piped the quails from shocks and sheaves,
And, like living coals, the apples Burned among the withering leaves.
HENRY WADSWORTH LONGFELLOW

• Swing the shining sickle,
Cut the ripening grain;
Gather in the harvest,
Fall is here again.
OLD SONG

• He that hath a good harvest may be content with some thistles.
ENGLISH PROVERB

• You sunburnt sickle men, of August weary,
Come hither from the furrow and be merry.
WILLIAM SHAKESPEARE

• Gather the gifts of earth with equal hand;
Henceforth ye, too, may share the birthright soil,
The corn, the wine, and all the harvest-home.
E.C. STEDMAN

• Come, ye thankful people, come;
Raise the song of Harvest-home;
All is safely gathered in,
Ere the winter storms begin.
HENRY ALFORD

• In harvest time, harvest folk, servants and all,
Should make altogether good cheer in the hall.
THOMAS TUSSER

• Live within your harvest.
PERSIUS

• Some are bumper harvests, and some don't do much more than get the seed back. It's like life. It all evens out.
RALPH HANSEN

• For the unlearned, old age is winter; for the learned, it is the season of the harvest.
THE TALMUD

• A harvest moon!/And on the mats—/Shadows of pine boughs.
KIKAKU

• Nobody can go through an endless chain of farm births and

growth and harvest—and be subject to Nature's mysteries, bounty, and sometimes harshness—without developing a philosophy of life.

MRS. J. BREWER BOTTORFF

• What is more cheerful, now, in the fall of the year, than an open wood fire? Do you hear those little chirps and twitters coming out of that piece of apple wood? Those are the ghosts of the robins and bluebirds that sang upon the bough when it was in blossom last spring.

THOMAS BAILEY ALDRICH

• And when ye reap the harvest of your land, thou shalt not wholly reap the corners of thy field, neither shalt thou gather the gleanings of thy harvest.

And thou shalt not glean thy vineyard, neither shalt thou gather every grape of thy vineyard; thou shalt leave them for the poor and stranger.

LEVITICUS 19. 9-10

• Life's field will yield as we make it—a harvest of thorns or of flowers.

UNKNOWN

• The only act of infidelity for which Papa could have ever been accused and found guilty was a love affair with Mother Earth. And yet she could dash his hopes, change his mind, defeat his purposes. He loved her with a passion, and his greatest moments of triumph, his highest achievements, were those times when she would return a harvest so bountiful his barns couldn't hold it.

EARL GOOLSBY

• Now, God comes to thee, not as in the dawning of the day, not as in the bud of the spring, but as the sun at noon to illustrate all shadows, as the sheaves in harvest, to fill all penuries; all occasions invite his mercies, and all times are his seasons.

JOHN DONNE

• If you would reap praise, you must sow the Seeds, gentle Words and useful Deeds.

BENJAMIN FRANKLIN

Wealth

Even adults have a hard time distinguishing needs from wants. For children, it's harder still. One dad explained it this way to his two youngsters: "You may not have everything you want, but you have everything you need." And sometimes that's a lot less than we think.

• The best thing a man can do for his culture when he is rich is to endeavor to carry out those schemes which he entertained when he was poor.

HENRY DAVID THOREAU

• Wealth maketh many friends.

PROVERBS 19: 4

• If a man runs after money, he's money-mad; if he keeps it, he's a capitalist; if he spends it, he's a playboy; if he doesn't get it, he's a ne'er-do-well; if he doesn't try to get it, he lacks ambition. If he gets it without working for it, he's a parasite; and if he accumulates it after a lifetime of hard work, people call him a fool who never got anything out of life.

VIC OLIVER

• His best companions, innocence and health;/And his best riches, ignorance of wealth.

OLIVER GOLDSMITH

• Get what you can and keep what you have. That's the way to get rich.

SCOTTISH PROVERB

• The easiest way to live within your income is to have a big one.

UNKNOWN

• Wealth is the means, and people are the ends. All our material riches will avail us little if we do not use them to expand the opportunities of our people.

JOHN FITZGERALD KENNEDY

• I wish to become rich, so that I can instruct the people and glorify honest poverty a little, like those kind-hearted, fat, benevolent people do.

MARK TWAIN

• There is no road to wealth so easy and respectable as that of matrimony.

ANTHONY TROLLOPE

• The boast of heraldry, the pomp of pow'r,/And all that beauty, all that wealth e'er gave,/Awaits alike the inevitable hour;/The paths of glory lead but to the grave.

THOMAS GRAY

• The seven deadly sins . . . food, clothing, firing, rent, taxes, respectability, and children. Nothing can lift those seven millstones from man's neck but money; and the spirit cannot soar until the millstones are lifted.

GEORGE BERNARD SHAW

• To really enjoy the better things in life, one must first have experienced the things they are better than.

OSCAR HOMOLKA

• Poverty is no disgrace to a man, but it is confoundedly inconvenient.

SYDNEY SMITH

• There are a handful of people whom money won't spoil, and we count ourselves among them.

MIGNON MCLAUGHLIN

• For thy sweet love remembered such wealth brings/That then I scorn to change my state with kings.

WILLIAM SHAKESPEARE

• The company of just and righteous men is better than wealth and a rich estate.

EURIPIDES

• When a fellow says, "It ain't the money but the principle of the thing," it's the money.

KIN HUBBARD

• Surplus wealth is a sacred trust, which its possessor is bound to administer in his lifetime for the good of the community.

ANDREW CARNEGIE

• Money is what you'd get on beautifully without if only other people weren't so crazy about it.

MARGARET CASE HARRIMAN

• Misers aren't fun to live with, but they make wonderful ancestors.

DAVID BRENNER

• The love of wealth is therefore to be traced, as either a principal or accessory motive, at the bottom of all that the Americans do; this gives to all their passions a sort of family likeness. . . . It may be said that it is the vehemence of their desires that makes the Americans so methodical; it perturbs their minds, but it disciplines their lives.

ALEXIS DE TOCQUEVILLE

• How much money is enough?

THE TALMUD

Persistence

Among some skaters was a small boy so obviously a beginner that his frequent tumbles awakened the pity of a tenderhearted, if not wise, spectator. "Why, child," she said, "I wouldn't stay on the ice and keep falling down; I'd just come off and watch the others." Quickly brushing away his tears, the little fellow looked from his advisor to the shining blades on his feet and answered indignantly, "I didn't get new skates to give up with; I got them to learn how with."

• Success is to be measured not so much by the position that one has reached in life as by the obstacles that he has overcome while trying to succeed.

BOOKER T. WASHINGTON

• No matter how bad things get, you got to go on living, even if it kills you.

SHOLOM ALEICHEM

• Life will give you what you ask of her if only you ask long enough and plainly enough.

EDITH NESBIT

• I know of no more encouraging fact than the unquestionable ability of man to elevate his life by a conscious endeavor.

HENRY DAVID THOREAU

• Big shots are only little shots who keep on shooting.

CHRISTOPHER MORLEY

• Behold, we count them happy which endure.

JAMES 5: 11

• Let a man begin with an earnest "I ought," and if he perseveres, by God's grace he will end in the free blessedness of "I will."

F. W. ROBERTSON

• Even after a bad harvest, there must be sowing.

SENECA

• The rung of a ladder was never meant to rest upon, but only to hold a man's foot long enough to enable him to put the other somewhat higher.

THOMAS HENRY HUXLEY

• Consider the postage stamp, my son. It secures success through its ability to stick to one thing till it gets there.

JOSH BILLINGS

• I believe that man will not merely endure; he will prevail. He is immortal, not because he alone among creatures has an inexhaustible voice, but because he has a soul, a spirit capable of compassion and sacrifice and endurance.

WILLIAM FAULKNER

• The difference between perseverance and obstinacy is that one often comes from a strong will, and the other from a strong won't.

HENRY WARD BEECHER

• The conditions of conquest are always easy. We have but to toil awhile, endure awhile, believe always, and never turn back.

WILLIAM GILMORE SIMMS

• Life only demands from the strength you possess. Only one feat is possible—not to have run away.

DAG HAMMARSKJØLD

• I hold a doctrine, to which I owe not much, indeed, but all the little I ever had, namely, that with ordinary talent and extraordinary perseverance, all things are attainable.

T.F. BUXTON

• There is no royal road to anything. One thing at a time, and all things in succession. That which grows slowly, endures.

J.G. HOLLAND

• Let me tell you the secret that has led me to my goal. My strength lies solely in my tenacity.

LOUIS PASTEUR

• There is no failure except in no longer trying. There is no defeat except from within, no really insurmountable barrier save our own inherent weakness of purpose.

KIN HUBBARD

• To persevere, trusting in what hopes he has, is courage in a man. The coward despairs.

EURIPIDES

• Never give in, never give in, never, never, never, never.

WINSTON CHURCHILL

• If a man has any brains at all, let him hold on to his calling, and, in the grand sweep of things, his turn will come at last.

WILLIAM C. McCUNE

• Keep on going and chances are you will stumble on something, perhaps when you are least expecting it. I have never heard of anyone stumbling on something sitting down.

CHARLES F. KETTERING

• Nothing in this world can take the place of persistence. Talent will not; nothing is more common than unsuccessful men with talent. The slogan "press on" has solved and always will solve the problems of the race.

CALVIN COOLIDGE

Enthusiasm

Think about the most enthusiastic person you know. You kinda like being around that person, don't you? 'Nuff said.

• The vitality of thought is in adventure. *Ideas won't keep.* Something must be done about them. When the idea is new, its custodians have fervor, live for it, and, if need be, die for it.

ALFRED NORTH WHITEHEAD

• Nothing great was ever achieved without enthusiasm.

RALPH WALDO EMERSON

• Through zeal, knowledge is gotten; through lack of zeal, knowledge is lost; let a man who knows this double path of gain and loss thus place himself that knowledge may grow.

BUDDHA

• Nature drives with a loose rein, and vitality of any sort can blunder through many a predicament in which reason would despair.

GEORGE SANTAYANA

• Have a purpose in life, and having it, throw into your work such strength of mind and muscle as God has given you.

THOMAS CARLYLE

• The wise and active conquer difficulties by daring to attempt them. Sloth and folly shiver and shrink at sight of toil and hazard, and make the impossibility they fear.

NICHOLAS ROWE

• Years wrinkle the skin, but lack of enthusiasm wrinkles the soul.

UNKNOWN

• Whatsoever thy hand findeth to do, do it with thy might; for there is no work, nor device, nor knowledge, nor wisdom in the grave, whither thou goest.

ECCLESIASTES 9: 10

• One hour of life, crowded to the full with glorious action, and filled with noble risks, is worth whole years of those mean observances of paltry decorum.

WALTER SCOTT

• The most absurd and reckless aspirations have sometimes led to extraordinary success.

MARQUIS DE VAUVENARGUES

• I love enthusiasts; exalted people frighten me.

JOSEPH ROUX

• There are important cases in which the difference between half a heart and a whole heart makes just the difference between signal defeat and a splendid victory.

A.H.K. BOYD

• Enthusiasm is that temper of the mind in which the imagination has got the better of the judgment.

BISHOP WILLIAM WARBURTON

• To do anything in this world worth doing, we must not stand back shivering and thinking of the cold and danger, but jump in, and scramble through as well as we can.

SYDNEY SMITH

• Nothing is so contagious as enthusiasm. It is the real allegory of the tale of Orpheus; it moves stones, and charms brutes. It is the genius of sincerity, and truth accomplishes no victories without it.

JOHN BULWER

• No wild enthusiast ever yet could rest, till half mankind were, like himself, possessed.

WILLIAM COWPER

• The main dangers in this life are the people who want to change everything—or nothing.

LADY ASTOR

• Enthusiasm is a virtue rarely to be met with in seasons of calm and unruffled prosperity. It flourishes in adversity, kindles in the hour of danger, and awakens to deeds of renown. The terrors of persecution only serve to quicken the energy of its purposes. It swells in proud integrity, and, great in the purity of its cause, it can scatter defiance amidst hosts of enemies.

THOMAS CHALMERS

• Exuberance is Beauty.

WILLIAM BLAKE

Taxes

Whether rendering unto Caesar or anteing up to Uncle Sam, most of us contribute (usually without joy) to the financial coffers that help support governments. Actually, there is nothing wrong with taxes that a good boost in income wouldn't solve.

• We are taxed twice as much by our idleness, three times as much by our pride, and four times as much by our folly; and from these taxes the commissioners cannot ease or deliver us by allowing an abatement.

BENJAMIN FRANKLIN

• The corruption of democracies proceeds directly from the fact that one class imposes the taxes and another class pays them. The constitutional principle, "No taxation without representation," is utterly set at naught.

W.R. INGE

• That the power to tax involves also the power to destroy [is] not to be denied.

JOHN MARSHALL, FORMER CHIEF JUSTICE

• Those who can do a good trade don't wrangle over taxes.

WILLIAM SCARBOROUGH

• It is the part of a good shepherd to shear the flock, not flay it.

TIBERIUS CAESAR

• The art of taxation consists in so plucking the goose as to obtain the largest possible amount of feathers with the smallest possible amount of hissing.

JEAN BAPTISTE COLBERT

• The income tax has made liars out of more Americans than golf.

WILL ROGERS

• There is one difference between a tax collector and a taxidermist: the taxidermist leaves the hide.

MORTIMER CAPLAN

• The point to remember is that what the government gives it must first take away.

JOHN S. COLEMAN

• Man is not like other animals in the ways that are really significant: animals have instinct, we have taxes.

ERVING GOFFMAN

• The trouble with being a breadwinner nowadays is that the government is in for such a big slice.

MARY MCCOY

• Taxes, after all, are the dues that we pay for the privileges of membership in an organized society.

FRANKLIN D. ROOSEVELT

• Next to being shot at and missed, nothing is quite as satisfying as an income tax refund.

F.J. RAYMOND

• Taxation with representation ain't so hot either.

GERALD BARZAN

• No matter how bad a child is, he is still good for a tax deduction.

AMERICAN PROVERB

• Make use of a costly vessel today, and enjoy it, for it may be taken from you tomorrow.

THE TALMUD

• The way taxes are, you might as well marry for love.

JOE E. LEWIS

• The only thing that hurts more than paying an income tax is not having to pay an income tax.

LORD THOMAS R. DUWAR

• We are not the bosses of taxpayers; they are ours.

T. COLEMAN ANDREWS, IRS DIRECTOR, 1955

• Few of us ever test our powers of deduction, except when filling out an income tax form.

GIL STERN

• Blessed are the young, for they shall inherit the national debt.

HERBERT HOOVER

• The reward of energy, enterprise, and thrift—is taxes.

WILLIAM FEATHER

• Why does a slight tax increase cost you $200 and a substantial tax cut save you 30 cents?

PEG BRACKEN

• Capital punishment: the income tax.

JEFF HAYES

• Anybody has a right to evade taxes if he can get away with it. No citizen has a moral obligation to assist in maintaining the government.

J. PIERPONT MORGAN

• Why shouldn't the American people take half my money from me? I took all of it from them.

EDWARD A. FILENE

• Auditors are the people who go in after the war is lost and bayonet the wounded.

P. RUBIN

15

Curiosity

Like most human qualities, curiosity has both negative and positive faces. The inquiring mind may be merely snooping with intent to meddle, or it may be experiencing that wholesome, lively interest that leads to sometimes startling and important new ideas, even to key discoveries.

• The first and simplest emotion which we discover in the human mind is curiosity.

EDMUND BURKE

• Talk of mysteries! Think of our life in Nature—daily to be shown matter, to come in contact with it—rocks, trees, wind on our cheeks! The solid earth! The actual world!

HENRY DAVID THOREAU

• An intelligent mind acquires knowledge, and the ear of the wise seeks knowledge.

PROVERBS 18: 15

• There are different kinds of curiosity; one of interest, which causes us to learn that which would be useful to us; and the other of pride, which springs from a desire to know that of which others are ignorant.

FRANÇOIS, DUC DE ROCHEFOUCAULD

• If a child is to keep alive his unborn sense of wonder without any such gift from the fairies, he needs the companionship of at least one adult who can share it, rediscovering with him the joy, excitement, and mystery of the world we live in.

RACHEL CARSON

• Enquire not what boils in another's pot.

THOMAS FULLER

• The universe is like a safe to which there is a combination, but the combination is locked up in the safe.

PETER DE VRIES

• Avoid him who, for mere curiosity, asks three questions running about a thing that cannot interest him.

JOHN CASPAR LAVATER

• Seize the moment of excited curiosity on any subject to solve your doubts; for if you let it pass, the desire may never return, and you may remain in ignorance.

WILLIAM WIRT

• A spirit of inquiry is the great characteristic of the age we live in.

JOHN POOLE

• He that pryeth into every cloud may be struck with a thunderbolt.

JOHN RAY

• Curiosity is one of the most permanent and certain characteristics of a vigorous intellect.

SAMUEL JOHNSON

• Deep in their roots,/All flowers keep the light.

THEODORE ROETHKE

• Curiosity can do more things than kill a cat.

O. HENRY

• Curiosity may have killed the cat, but it has never been detrimental to the doctor.

P.J. STEINCHROHN

• He has been that way for years—a born questioner—but he hates answers.

RING LARDNER

• By nature's kindly disposition most questions which it is beyond man's power to answer do not occur to him at all.

GEORGE SANTAYANA

• Curiosity has a spiteful way of turning back on the curious.

DOROTHY DISNEY

• Some people have an unconquerable love of riddles. They may have the chance of listening to plain sense, or to such wisdom as explains life; but no, they must go and work their brains over a riddle, just because they do not understand what it means.

ISAK DINESEN

• Newspapers always excite curiosity. No one ever lays one down without a feeling of disappointment.

CHARLES LAMB

• One demanding how God employed Himself before the world was made had answer: that He was making Hell for curious questioners.

JOHN MILTON

• Curiosity is little more than another name for hope.

J.C. AND A.W. HARE

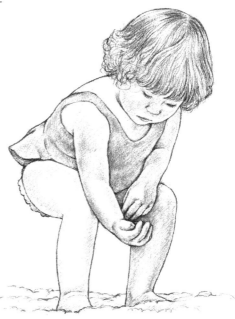

Experience

The little girl watched as her Daddy brought the pan of water to boil. She said, "Boy, Daddy, that looks hot. Why don't you put your finger in and see?" Without thinking, he did. Sometimes, even experience doesn't prevent you from making the same mistake again.

• Experience is a hard teacher because she gives the test first, the lesson afterwards.

VERNON SANDERS LAW

• If we shake hands with icy fingers, it is because we have burnt them so horribly before.

LOGAN PEARSALL SMITH

• He who has been bitten by a snake fears a piece of string.

PERSIAN PROVERB

• A proverb is no proverb to you till life has illustrated it.

JOHN KEATS

• Our whole past experience is continually in our consciousness, though most of it is sunk to a great depth of dimness. I think of consciousness as a vast bottomless lake, whose waters seem transparent, yet into which we can clearly see but a little way.

CHARLES SANDERS PEIRCE

• . . . I have learned by experience that the Lord has blessed me. . . .

GENESIS 30: 27

• When choosing between two evils, I always like to take the one I've never tried before.

MAE WEST

• I have never let my schooling interfere with my education.

MARK TWAIN

• You don't learn to hold your own in the world by standing on guard, but by attacking and getting well hammered yourself.

GEORGE BERNARD SHAW

• Life is like playing a violin in public, and learning the instrument as one goes on.

SAMUEL BUTLER

• Experience is what enables you to recognize a mistake when you make it again.

EARL WILSON

• Second marriage: The triumph of hope over experience.

SAMUEL JOHNSON

• A man never wakes up his second baby just to see it smile.

GRACE WILLIAMS

• Nothing is a waste of time if you use the experience wisely.

AUGUSTE RODIN

• Deep experience is never peaceful.

HENRY JAMES

• All experience is an arch wherethrough/Gleams that untravelled world whose margin fades/For ever and for ever when I move.

ALFRED, LORD TENNYSON

• I don't think much of a man who is not wiser today than he was yesterday.

ABRAHAM LINCOLN (WHEN CHARGED WITH HAVING CHANGED HIS MIND)

• I am not young enough to know everything.

OSCAR WILDE

• You must not think, sir, to catch old birds with chaff.

CERVANTES

• One thorn of experience is worth more than a whole wilderness of warning.

JAMES RUSSELL LOWELL

• Good judgment comes from experience, and experience—well, that comes from poor judgment.

UNKNOWN

• It's no use growing older if you only learn new ways of misbehaving yourself.

H.H. MUNRO

• One sees things for the first time only once.

THEODORE H. WHITE

• The wisdom of the wise and the experience of the ages are perpetuated by quotations.

BENJAMIN DISRAELI

Family

For most of us, the mention of family brings back fond memories of a distant past—of times so good that they overshadow the difficulties. Home is the place where we can go when we're tired and lonely; it is here in the family that we can be ourselves and still know we're accepted.

• Romance fails us and so do friendships, but the relationship of parent and child . . . remains indelible and indestructible, the strongest relationship on earth.
THEODOR REIK

• Home is not where you live but where they understand you.
CHRISTIAN MORGENSTERN

• You don't raise heroes, you raise sons. And if you treat them like sons, they'll turn out to be heroes, even if it's just in your own eyes.
WALTER SCHIRRA, SR.

• One characteristic of a strong family is that they find and focus on some positive element of a bad situation—something that will give them hope.
NICK STINNETT

• Let there be spaces in your togetherness.
KAHLIL GIBRAN

• I have come back again to where I belong; not an enchanted place, but the walls are strong.
DOROTHY H. RATH

• By and large, mothers and housewives are the only workers who do not have regular time off. They are the great vacationless class.
ANNE MORROW LINDBERGH

• The more people have studied different methods of bringing up children, the more they have come to the conclusion that what good mothers and fathers instinctively feel like doing for their babies is the best after all.
BENJAMIN SPOCK

• Heredity is nothing but stored environment.
LUTHER BURBANK

• A man's rootage is more important than his leafage.
WOODROW WILSON

• The man who has not anything to boast of but his illustrious ancestors is like a potato—the only good belonging to him is under ground.

THOMAS OVERBURY

• A wise son maketh a glad father: but a foolish son is the heaviness of his mother.

PROVERBS 10: 1

• No matter how many communes anybody invents, the family always creeps back.

MARGARET MEAD

• No one like one's mother and father ever lived.

ROBERT T.S. LOWELL

• All happy families resemble one another; every unhappy family is unhappy in its own way.

LEO TOLSTOY

• To bring up a child in the way he should go, travel that way yourself once in a while.

JOSH BILLINGS

• What children hear at home soon flies abroad.

THOMAS FULLER

• Families break up when people take hints you don't intend and miss hints you do intend.

ROBERT FROST

• Keep your eyes wide open before marriage, half shut afterwards.

BENJAMIN FRANKLIN

• Children are more powerful than oil, more beautiful than rivers, more precious than any other natural resource.

DANNY KAYE

• I have found the best way to give advice to your children is to find out what they want and then advise them to do it.

HARRY S. TRUMAN

• Sacred and happy homes . . . are the surest guarantees for the moral progress of a nation.

HENRY DRUMMOND

• The thorns which I have reaped are of the tree I planted.

LORD BYRON

• The root of the kingdom is in the state. The root of the state is in the family. The root of the family is in the person of its head.

MENCIUS

21

Democracy

"We hold these truths to be self-evident, that all men are created equal, that they are endowed by their Creator with certain inalienable rights, that among these are life, liberty, and the pursuit of happiness." Wonderful words, important words, but read them carefully. The establishment of these rights as well as the burden of maintaining them is the responsibility of the people, not the government.

• Democracy is being able to say no to the boss.

ALDOUS HUXLEY

• Many people consider the things which government does for them to be social progress, but they consider the things government does for others as socialism.

EARL WARREN, FORMER CHIEF JUSTICE

• Government is too big and important to be left to the politicians.

CHESTER BOWLES

• Man's capacity for justice makes democracy possible, but man's inclination to injustice makes democracy necessary.

REINHOLD NIEBUHR

• The idea that you can merchandise candidates for high office like breakfast cereal . . . is the ultimate indignity to the democratic process.

ADLAI STEVENSON

• If one man offers you democracy and another offers you a bag of grain, at what stage of starvation will you prefer the grain to the vote?

BERTRAND RUSSELL

• A nation may lose its liberties in a day and not miss them for a century.

BARON DE MONTESQUIEU

• Did you ever get the feeling that the only reason we have elections is to find out if the polls were right?

ROBERT ORBEN

• Democracy is based on the conviction that man has the moral and intellectual capacity, as well as the inalienable right, to govern himself with reason and justice.

HARRY S. TRUMAN

• They that can give up essential liberty to obtain a little temporary safety deserve neither liberty nor safety.

BENJAMIN FRANKLIN

• If you want to understand democracy, spend less time in the library with Plato and more time in the buses with people.

SIMEON STRUNSKY

• That government of the people, by the people, for the people, shall not perish from the earth.

ABRAHAM LINCOLN

• People often say that, in a democracy, decisions are made by a majority of the people. Of course, that is not true. Decisions are made by a majority of those who make themselves heard and who vote—a very different thing.

WALTER H. JUDD

• Whenever any form of government becomes destructive . . . it is the right of the people to alter or abolish it.

THE DECLARATION OF INDEPENDENCE

• Even though counting heads is not an ideal way to govern, at least it is better than breaking them.

LEARNED HAND

• Every government degenerates when trusted to the rulers of the people alone. The people themselves, therefore, are its only safe depositories.

THOMAS JEFFERSON

• One of the evils of democracy is, you have to put up with the man you elect whether you want him or not.

WILL ROGERS

• Sure the people are stupid; the human race is stupid. Sure Congress is an inefficient instrument of government. But the people are not stupid enough to abandon representative government for any other kind, including government by the guy who knows.

BERNARD DE VOTO

• Of the many things we have done to democracy in the past, the worst has been the indignity of taking it for granted.

MAX LERNER

• Those who profess to favor freedom, and yet depreciate agitation, are men who want rain without thunder and lightning.

FREDERICK DOUGLASS

• The progress of democracy seems irresistible, because it is the most uniform, the most ancient, and the most permanent tendency which is to be found in history.

ALEXIS DE TOCQUEVILLE

Courage

In the children's fantasy book The Wonderful Wizard of Oz, the Cowardly Lion becomes brave simply by believing that he has been given courage. But courage cannot be given or taken away. Instead, it is a trait inherent in everyone. Whether or not it is used is another story.

• Bravery is being the only one who knows you're afraid.
FRANKLIN P. JONES

• A timid person is frightened before a danger, a coward during the time, and a courageous person afterwards.
JEAN PAUL RICHTER

• It is to the interest of the commonwealth of mankind that there should be someone who is unconquered, someone against whom fortune has no power.
SENECA

• Perfect valor is to do unwitnessed what we should be capable of doing before all the world.
FRANÇOIS, DUC DE ROCHEFOUCAULD

• It is a blessed thing that in every age someone has had individuality enough and courage enough to stand by his own convictions.
ROBERT G. INGERSOLL

• If God wanted us to be brave, why did he give us legs?
MARVIN KITMAN

• We must have courage to bet on our ideas, to take the calculated risk, and to act. Everyday living requires courage if life is to be effective and bring happiness.
MAXWELL MALTZ

• He was a bold man who first swallowed an oyster.
JAMES I

• No man in the world has more courage than the man who can stop after eating one peanut.
CHANNING POLLOCK

• Cowards die many times before their deaths; the valiant never taste of death but once.
WILLIAM SHAKESPEARE

• Many become brave when brought to bay.
NORWEGIAN PROVERB

• O God, give us serenity to accept what cannot be changed; courage to change what should be changed; and wisdom to distinguish the one from the other.
REINHOLD NIEBUHR

• Courage is fear holding on a minute longer.
GEORGE S. PATTON

• Never let your head hang down. Never give up and sit down and grieve. Find another way. And don't pray when it rains if you don't pray when the sun shines.
SATCHEL PAIGE

• If one is forever cautious, can one remain a human being?
ALEXANDER SOLZHENITSYN

• The Ancient Mariner said to Neptune during a great storm, "O God, you will save me if you wish, but I am going to go on holding my tiller straight."
MONTAIGNE

• Fight on, my merry men all, / I'm a little wounded, but I am not slain; / I will lay me down for to bleed a while, / Then I'll rise and fight with you again.
JOHN DRYDEN

• A man does what he must—in spite of personal consequences, in spite of obstacles and dangers and pressures—and that is the basis of all morality.
JOHN FITZGERALD KENNEDY

• We must never despair; our situation has been compromising before, and it has changed for the better; so I trust it will again.
GEORGE WASHINGTON

• Then David took his staff in his hand, and chose five smooth stones from the brook, and put them in his shepherd's bag, in his wallet; his sling was in his hand, and he drew near to the Philistine.
I SAMUEL 17: 40

• One doesn't discover new lands without consenting to lose sight of the shore for a very long time.
ANDRE GIDÉ

Excellence

Fascinated, the young boy sat on the stool, watching his grand-mother knit a shawl. She deftly handled the two long needles while softly humming "Rock of Ages." Suddenly, she laid down her needles, grabbed the end of the yarn, and pulled out nearly 20 rows of stitches. Astonished, the young boy asked, "Grandma, why did you do that?" "Because I made a mistake," she replied and showed her grandson where she had missed a stitch. He could barely see the missed stitch. "Others may not notice the mistake," she said, "but I would always know."

• There is always a best way of doing everything, even if it be to boil an egg.

RALPH WALDO EMERSON

• Quality is not an act. It is a habit.

ARISTOTLE

• Trifles make perfection, and perfection is no trifle.

MICHELANGELO

• Everyone has a mass of bad work in him which he will have to work off and get rid of before he can do better; and, indeed, the more lasting a man's ultimate work, the more sure he is to pass through a time, and perhaps a very long one, in which there seems to be very little hope for him.

SAMUEL BUTLER

• Consider first, that great/Or bright infers not excellence.

JOHN MILTON

• A man is valued as he makes himself valuable.

F.E. HULME

• Life is strange. Every so often a good man wins.

FRANK DANE

• The closest to perfection a person ever comes is when he fills out a job application form.

STANLEY J. RANDALL

• One machine can do the work of 50 ordinary men. No machine can do the work of 1 extraordinary man.

ELBERT HUBBARD

• Give me a lever long enough and a fulcrum strong enough, and singlehanded I can move the world.

ARCHIMEDES

• There are no perfect men, of course, but some are more perfect than others, and we can use all of those we can get.

MERLE SHAIN

• Nothing is such an obstacle to the production of excellence as the power of producing what is good with ease and rapidity.

JOHN AIKIN

• If you wish your merit to be known, acknowledge that of other people.

ORIENTAL PROVERB

• There is none who cannot teach somebody something, and there is none so excellent but he is ex-celled.

BALTASAR GRACIÁ

• If a man aspires to the highest place, it is no dishonor to him to halt at the second, or even the third.

CICERO

• Virtue and genuine graces in themselves speak what no words can utter.

WILLIAM SHAKESPEARE

• He who is slack in his work is a brother to him who destroys.

PROVERBS 18: 9

• Our merit wins the esteem of honest men, and our lucky star that of the public.

FRANÇOIS, DUC DE ROCHEFOUCAULD

• It never occurs to fools that merit and good fortune are closely united.

JOHANN WOLFGANG VON GOETHE

• The renown which riches or beauty confer is fleeting and frail; mental excellence is a splendid and lasting possession.

SALLUST

• Too low they build who build beneath the stars.

OWEN D. YOUNG

• It takes a long time to bring excellence to maturity.

LIVY

• The finite mind does not require to grasp the infinitude of truth, but only to go forward from light to light.

PETER BAYNE

• Different men excel in different ways.

PINDAR

Indecision

Don't let fear paralyze you with indecision. Get the facts. Look at the best- and worst-case scenarios. Then, make your decision. He who hesitates is lost and usually forgotten.

• First you say you do, and then you don't. / And then you say you will, and then you won't. / You're undecided now, so what are you gonna do?
SID ROBIN

• I'll give you a definite maybe.
SAMUEL GOLDWYN

• To be always intending to live a new life, but never to find time to set about it, this is as if a man should put off eating, drinking, and sleeping from one day and night to another till he is starved and destroyed.
JOHN TILLOTSON

• It is a miserable thing to live in suspense; it is the life of a spider.
JONATHAN SWIFT

• I must have a prodigious quantity of mind; it takes me as much as a week, sometimes, to make it up.
MARK TWAIN

• Take time to deliberate, but when the time for action arrives, stop thinking and go in.
ANDREW JACKSON

• It is a great evil, as well as a misfortune, to be unable to utter a prompt and decided "no."
CHARLES SIMMONS

• Nothing is more difficult, and therefore more precious, than to be able to decide.
NAPOLEON BONAPARTE

• There is nothing in the world more pitiable than an irresolute man.
JOHANN WOLFGANG VON GOETHE

• When a man has not a good reason for doing a thing, he has one good reason for letting it alone.
THOMAS SCOTT

• A man without decision can never be said to belong to himself; he is as a wave of the sea, or a feather in the air, which every breeze blows about as it listeth.
JOHN FOSTER

• If it be right, do it boldly. If it be wrong, leave it undone.
BERNARD GILPIN

• There will always be someone who will oppose every decision you make.
UNKNOWN

• The block of granite, which was an obstacle in the pathway of the weak, becomes a stepping-stone in the pathway of the strong.
THOMAS CARLYLE

• The man who has not learned to say "no" will be a weak if not a wretched man as long as he lives.
ALEXANDER MACLAREN

• When in doubt, duck.
MALCOLM FORBES

• Decide not rashly. The decision made can never be recalled.
HENRY WADSWORTH LONGFELLOW

• Major decisions usually require predictions about the future.
HARRY A. BULLIS

• Half the failures in life arise from pulling in one's horse as he is leaping.
J.C. AND A.W. HARE

• Indecision is like the stepchild: If he doesn't wash his hands, he is called dirty; if he does, he is wasting the water.
MADAGASCAN PROVERB

• No wind serves him who addresses his voyage to no certain port.
MONTAIGNE

• Don't stand shivering upon the bank; plunge in at once, and have it over.
SAM SLICK

• Give your decisions, never your reasons. Your decisions may be right, your reasons are sure to be wrong.
WILLIAM MURRAY, EARL OF MANSFIELD

• The desire to remain popular has influenced too many business decisions.
HERMAN W. STEINKRAUS

• Formulate your feelings as well as your thoughts.
A.R. ORAGE

Failure

He lost his ranch. He lost his new car dealership. Now, he's selling used cars in a small rural town. Oh, there were plenty of reasons—high interest rates, the depressed rural economy, and so on. "I've got a loving wife and a wonderful family, and I just became a grandpa. If this makes me a failure, then so be it," he says.

• We can't all be heroes because somebody has to sit on the curb and clap as they go by.
WILL ROGERS

• There is much to be said for failure. It is more interesting than success.
MAX BEERBOHM

• The first and great commandment is, "Don't let them scare you."
ELMER DAVIS

• Never show your wounded finger.
BALTASAR GRACIAN

• Every day cannot be a feast of lanterns.
CHINESE PROVERB

• There is the greatest practical benefit in making a few failures early in life.
THOMAS HENRY HUXLEY

• Nothing is more humiliating than to see idiots succeed in enterprises we have failed in.
GUSTAVE FLAUBERT

• What is defeat? Nothing but education, nothing but the first step to something better.
WENDELL PHILLIPS

• No one can make you feel inferior without your consent.
ELEANOR ROOSEVELT

• I would prefer even to fail with honor than to win by cheating.
SOPHOCLES

• The mistakes are all there waiting to be made.
TARTAKOWER, CHESSMASTER

• Flops are a part of life's menu, and I've never been a girl to miss out on any of the courses.
ROSALIND RUSSELL

• The folly of one man is the fortune of another.
FRANCIS BACON

- The girl who can't dance says the band can't play.
YIDDISH PROVERB

- We are all failures—at least the best of us are.
JAMES M. BARRIE

- Nothing is impossible for the person who doesn't have to do it.
WELLER'S LAW

- A word of encouragement during a failure is worth more than a whole book of praise after a success.
UNKNOWN

- The doctor can bury his mistakes, but an architect can only advise his client to plant vines.
FRANK LLOYD WRIGHT

- He who would have the fruit must climb the tree.
THOMAS FULLER

- Fear of becoming a has-been keeps some people from becoming anything.
ERIC HOFFER

- In the future, everyone will be world-famous for 15 minutes.
ANDY WARHOL

- By the time we've made it, we've had it.
MALCOM FORBES

- We are not interested in the possibilities of defeat.
QUEEN VICTORIA

- No man is a failure who is enjoying life.
WILLIAM FEATHER

- Just think how happy you would be if you lost everything you have right now and then got it back.
FRANCES RODMAN

- When we do the best that we can, we never know what miracle is wrought in our life, or in the life of another.
HELEN KELLER

- Every exit is an entry somewhere else.
TOM STOPPARD

Truth

How do you prevent a child from lying? The same way you prevent a child from cursing, cheating, taking drugs, or any other unacceptable behavior—by your own example.

• Every truth passes through three stages before it is recognized. In the first it is ridiculed; in the second it is opposed; in the third it is regarded as self-evident.

ARTHUR SCHOPENHAUER

• A truth that's told with bad intent/Beats all the lies you can invent.

WILLIAM BLAKE

• If you speak the truth, have a foot in the stirrup.

TURKISH PROVERB

• Pretty much all the honest truthtelling there is in the world is done by children.

UNKNOWN

• A thing is not necessarily true because a man dies for it.

OSCAR WILDE

• Experience has taught me, when the versions of the same story given by two wire services differ materially, to prefer the less exciting.

ELMER DAVIS

• Jesus answered, "To this end was I born, and for this cause came I into the world, that I should bear witness unto the truth."

JOHN 18: 37-38

• Falsehood is so near to truth that a wise man would do well not to trust himself on such a narrow edge.

CICERO

• Give a lie 24 hours' start, and you can never overtake it.

V.S. LEAN

• All men, as far as in them lies,/ Create realities of dreams;/To truth our nature proves but ice,/ To falsehood, fire it seems.

JEAN DE LA FONTAINE

• Men occasionally stumble over the truth, but most of them pick themselves up and hurry off as if nothing had happened.

WINSTON CHURCHILL

• For of course the true meaning of a term is to be found by observing what a man does with it, not by what he says about it.

P.W. BRIDGMAN

• It will not break, like a bubble, at a touch; nay, you may kick it about all day like a football, and it will be round and full at evening.

OLIVER WENDELL HOLMES

• Let us begin by committing ourselves to the truth–to see it like it is, and tell it like it is–to find the truth, to speak the truth, and to live the truth.

RICHARD M. NIXON

• The credibility gap is so wide that our suspicions are confirmed by any official denial.

LAURENCE J. PETER

• Say not, "I have found the truth," but rather, "I have found a truth."

KAHLIL GIBRAN

• It is dangerous for mortal beauty, or terrestrial virtue, to be examined by too strong a light.

SAMUEL JOHNSON

• Truth, like the juice of the poppy, in small quantities calms men; in larger, heats and irritates them and is attended by fatal consequences in its excess.

WALTER SAVAGE LANDOR

• If you believe everything you read, better not read.

JAPANESE PROVERB

• When an opinion is true, it may be extinguished once, twice, or many times, but in the course of ages there will generally be found persons to rediscover it.

JOHN STUART MILL

• There is nothing the matter with this, except that it ain't so.

MARK TWAIN

• Truth often suffers more by the heat of its defenders than from the arguments of its opposers.

WILLIAM PENN

• Men of business must not break their word twice.

THOMAS FULLER

• Nothing makes a man or body of men as mad as the truth. If there is no truth in it, they laugh it off.

WILL ROGERS

• I would sooner have you hate me for telling you the truth than adore me for telling you lies.

PIETRO ARETINO

Reading

"A B C D E F G H I J K L M N O P Q R S T U V W X Y Z. Now, I've said my ABC's. Tell me what you think of me." The ABC's are where reading begins. They're where we take our first hesitant steps toward contributing to the betterment of the human race. What do I think of you? A lot, a whole lot.

• Read the best books first, or you may not have a chance to read them at all.

HENRY DAVID THOREAU

• All good books are alike in that they are truer than if they had really happened and after you are finished reading one you will feel that all that happened to you and afterwards it all belongs to you: the good and the bad, the ecstasy, the remorse and the sorrow, the people and the places and how the weather was.

ERNEST HEMINGWAY

• A great writer is, so to speak, a second government in his country.

ALEXANDER SOLZHENITSYN

• The instruction we find in books is like fire. We fetch it from our neighbors, kindle it at home, communicate it to others, and it becomes the property of all.

VOLTAIRE

• Man's mind stretched by a new idea never goes back to its original dimensions.

OLIVER WENDELL HOLMES

• I think we ought to read only the kind of books that wound and stab us . . . . We heed the books that affect us like a disaster, that

grieve us deeply, like the death of someone we loved more than ourselves, like being banished into forests far from everyone, like a suicide. A book must be the axe for the frozen sea inside us.

FRANZ KAFKA

• There is nothing that strengthens a nation like [the] reading of a nation's own history, whether that history is recorded in books or embodied in customs, institutions, and monuments.

JOSEPH ANDERSON

• We should accustom the mind to keep the best company by introducing it only to the best books.

SYDNEY SMITH

• An ordinary man . . . can surround himself with 2,000 books . . . and thenceforward have at least one place in the world in which it is possible to be happy.

AUGUSTINE BIRRELL

• Reading is to the mind what exercise is to the body.

SIR RICHARD STEELE

• Some books are to be tasted, others to be swallowed, and some few to be digested.

FRANCIS BACON

• Be careful about reading health books. You may die of a misprint.

MARK TWAIN

• There are 70 million books in American libraries, but the one you want to read is always out.

TOM MASSON

• Never judge a book by its movie.

J.W. EAGAN

• I would sooner read a timetable or a catalog than nothing at all.

W. SOMERSET MAUGHAM

• Reading is a basic tool in the living of the good life.

MORTIMER J. ADLER

• I am a part of all I have read.

JOHN KIERAN

• When I am dead, I hope it may be said: "His sins were scarlet, but his books were read."

HILAIRE BELLOC

• In general, I like wedding bells at the end of novels. "They married and lived happily ever after"— why not? It has been done.

A. EDWARD NEWTON

• To sit alone in the lamplight with a book spread out before you, and hold intimate conversations—such is pleasure beyond compare.

YOSHIDA KENKO

• I have always imagined that Paradise will be a kind of library.

JORGE LUIS BORGES

Statistics

We are born, we live, we die. All our comings and goings are entered in the records of mankind—to be shuffled, categorized, studied, and interpreted. Our beliefs, work, ideas, and habits suffer the same scrutiny. Why are we so intent on measurements? Does gathering facts and putting them together improve our lives? Or is it possible that by focusing on the numbers, we're ignoring life itself?

• Do not put faith in what statistics say until you have carefully considered what they do not say.

WILLIAM W. WATT

• He uses statistics as a drunken man uses lampposts—for support rather than for illumination.

ANDREW LANG

• How far would Moses have gone if he had taken a poll in Egypt?

HARRY S. TRUMAN

• Science is facts; just as houses are made of stones, so is science made of facts; but a pile of stones is not a house and a collection of facts is not necessarily science.

HENRI POINCARÉ

• There are in the field of economic events no constant relations, and consequently no measurement is possible.

LUDWIG ELDER VON MISES

• Figures won't lie, but liars will figure.

CHARLES H. GROSVENOR

• Get your facts first, and then you can distort them as much as you please.

MARK TWAIN

• Our current addiction to pollsters and forecasters is a symptom of our chronic uncertainty about the future. Even when the forecasts prove wrong, we will go on asking for them. We watch our experts read the entrails of statistical tables and graphs the way the ancients watched their soothsayers read the entrails of a chicken.

ERIC HOFFER

• A single death is a tragedy; a million deaths is a statistic.

JOSEPH STALIN

• I shall always consider the best guesser the best prophet.

MARCUS TULLIUS CICERO

• Particulars are not to be examined till the whole has been surveyed.

EMANUEL CELLER

• I shall always consider the best guesser the best prophet.

MARCUS TULLIUS CICERO

• Situations are rarely ever black or white; they are usually varying shades of grey.

RAY E. BROWN

• A scientist is a man who would rather count than guess.

LEONARD LOUIS LEVINSON

• When you think you have obtained a reasonable percentage of the facts, try making a tentative decision and then see whether the evidence supports it.

HARRY A. BULLIS

• Prolonged statistics are a lethal dose, which if it does not kill will certainly dispel your audience.

ILKA CHASE

• I always find that statistics are hard to swallow and impossible to digest. The only one I can ever remember is that if all the people who go to sleep in church were laid end to end they would be a lot more comfortable.

MRS. ROBERT A. TAFT

• No one sees further into a generalization than his own knowledge of details extends.

WILLIAM JAMES

• There are three kinds of lies; lies, damned lies, and statistics.

BENJAMIN DISRAELI

• The facts, all we want is the facts.

SGT. JOE FRIDAY

• Job opens his mouth in empty talk, he multiplies words without knowledge.

JOB 35: 16

• An ounce of emotion is equal to a ton of facts.

JOHN JUNOR

• We think in generalities, but we live in detail.

ALFRED NORTH WHITEHEAD

• I could prove God statistically.

GEORGE GALLUP, JR.

CORNL

Humor

Having given man dominion over the earth, God probably decided He'd better throw in a sense of humor. Good thing too. For it is humor that makes us see the funny side of things—even when we don't much want to. It is humor that heals, invigorates, uplifts, and, in the words of Josh Billings (quoted below), lets us "laugh until the soul is thoroughly rested."

• God cannot be solemn, or he would not have blessed man with the incalculable gift of laughter.

SYDNEY HARRIS

• A person reveals his character by nothing so clearly as the joke he resents.

G.C. LICHTENBERG

• Humor is laughing at what you haven't got when you ought to have it.

LANGSTON HUGHES

• I like the laughter that opens the lips and the heart, that shows at the same time pearls and the soul.

VICTOR HUGO

• Any man will admit if need be that his sight is not good, or that he cannot swim or shoots badly with a rifle, but to touch upon his sense of humor is to give him mortal affront.

STEPHEN LEACOCK

• True humor springs not more from the head than from the heart; it is not contempt, its essence is love; it issues not in laughter, but in still smiles, which lie far deeper.

THOMAS CARLYLE

• There are very few good judges of humor, and they don't agree.

JOSH BILLINGS

• I live in a constant endeavor to fence against the infirmities of ill health and other evils of life by mirth. I am persuaded that every time a man smiles—but much more so when he laughs—it adds something to this fragment of life.

LAURENCE STERNE

• A man isn't poor if he can still laugh.

RAYMOND HITCHCOCK

• A satirist is a man who discovers unpleasant things about himself and then says them about other people.

PETER MCARTHUR

• To everything there is a season, and a time to every purpose under the heaven. . . . A time to weep, and a time to laugh; a time to mourn, and a time to dance.

ECCLESIASTES 3: 1, 4

• Life does not cease to be funny when people die any more than it ceases to be serious when people laugh.

GEORGE BERNARD SHAW

• If I had no sense of humor, I would long ago have committed suicide.

MAHATMA GANDHI

• No dignity, no learning, no force of character can make any stand against good wit.

RALPH WALDO EMERSON

• For health and the constant enjoyment of life, give me a keen and ever present sense of humor; it is the next best thing to an abiding faith in providence.

G.B. CHEEVER

• One loses so many laughs by not laughing at oneself.

SARA JEANNETTE DUNCAN

• The love of truth lies at the root of much humor.

ROBERTSON DAVIES

• It is the uncensored sense of humor . . . which is the ultimate therapy for man in society.

EVAN ESAR

• We are all here for a spell. Get all the good laughs you can.

WILL ROGERS

• If it's sanity you're after / There's no recipe like Laughter. / Laugh it off.

HENRY RUTHERFORD ELLIOT

• Humor is an affirmation of dignity, a declaration of man's superiority to all that befalls him.

ROMAIN GARY

• We must laugh at man to avoid crying for him.

NAPOLEON BONAPARTE

• Humor can be dissected, as a frog can, but the thing dies in the process.

E.B. WHITE

• The most utterly lost of all days is that in which you have not once laughed.

SEBASTIAN ROCH CHAMFORT

Superstition

Who me? Superstitious? You must be kidding. Hey, don't walk under that ladder. We may not walk around the block to keep a black cat from crossing our paths, but many of us will feel uneasy about it. Mark Twain said, "Let me make the superstitions of a nation, and I care not who makes its laws or its songs, either." Here are some common (and uncommon) superstitions.

• It is bad luck to watch a person out of sight. If you do, you will never see him again.

• Taking the left shoe off first is unlucky, as is putting your shoes on a table.

• When walking with a friend, you should never let an object like a post come between you. If it does, say "bread and butter" to avert bad luck or a quarrel.

• When two people wipe their hands at the same time, it means they will have a quarrel. They can avoid it by twisting the towel.

• To avoid misfortune, you should leave a house by the same door you used in entering it.

• If you give a knife to a friend as a gift, he must give you a present or a penny, or it will cut (end) your friendship.

• No dogs should be in the room where a poker game is being played, and the cards should not be picked up until the entire hand has been dealt.

• A dog crossing a ball field before the first pitch is sure to bring disaster to the team at bat.

• It's bad luck to change a garment that you have accidentally put on wrong side out.

• If the sun shines while it is raining, there will be rain again tomorrow at the same time.

• When the ass begins to bray, we surely shall have rain that day.

• It is unlucky to have an umbrella or a black suitcase on a ship.

• Feed a cold and starve a fever.

• If the right eye itches, you will rejoice; if the left, you will cry.

• Itching of the nose forebodes a quarrel, but itching of the palm indicates that money will be received.

• A person dies when he uses up the number of words allotted to him for his lifetime.

Kathryn Windham, an Alabama author known for her stories about ghosts, has collected these sayings about ways to deter evil spirits.

• Put a pair of shoes under your bed, one with the toe pointed out, one with the toe pointed in.

• Carry a buckeye in your pocket. Also, anyone who carries a buckeye in his pocket will never die drunk.

• Put empty bottles on the limbs of a tree in your yard. I once saw one covered with blue Milk of Magnesia bottles, and it was just beautiful.

• Sprinkle plain salt (iodized won't work) around your house.

• Dig a moat around your house and fill it with pure water.

• Take a white cotton rag, about 18 inches square, and wave it around your head as you run around your house three times. (Only pure materials will keep away evil spirits. Never put your faith in alloys or in synthetics.)

CORNL

Quality

The first symptom of complacency is satisfaction with things as they are. The second is a rejection of things as they might be. "Good enough" becomes today's watchword and tomorrow's standard. Complacency makes people fear the unknown, mistrust the untried, and abhor the new. Like water, those who are complacent follow the easiest course—downhill.

• Nothing great is created suddenly, any more than a bunch of grapes or a fig. If you tell me that you desire a fig, I answer you that there must be time. Let it first blossom, then bear fruit, then ripen.

EPICTETUS

• Whatever is worth doing at all, is worth doing well.

PHILIP DORMER STANHOPE

• I'm a great believer in luck, and I find the harder I work the more I have of it.

THOMAS JEFFERSON

• Once conform, once do what others do because they do it, and a kind of lethargy steals over all the finer senses of the soul.

MONTAIGNE

• When I was a young man, I observed that nine out of ten things I did were failures. I didn't want to be a failure, so I did ten times more work.

GEORGE BERNARD SHAW

• Indifference may not wreck a man's life at any one turn, but it will destroy him with a kind of dry rot in the long run.

BLISS CARMAN

• Once you say you're going to settle for second, that's what happens to you in life, I find.

JOHN FITZGERALD KENNEDY

• Ah, but a man's reach should exceed his grasp, or what's a heaven for?

ROBERT BROWNING

• Do what you can, with what you have, where you are.

THEODORE ROOSEVELT

• For a man to achieve all that is demanded of him he must regard himself as greater than he is.

JOHANN WOLFGANG VON GOETHE

• Every calling is great when greatly pursued.

OLIVER WENDELL HOLMES, JR.

• Greatness after all, in spite of its name, appears to be not so much a certain size as a certain quality in human lives. It may be present in lives whose range is very small.

PHILLIPS BROOKS

• One time, my son Patrick brought me a story and asked me to edit it for him. I went over it carefully and changed one word. "But, Papa," he said, "you've only changed one word." I said: "If it's the right word, that's a lot."

ERNEST HEMINGWAY

• If you would hit the mark, you must aim a little above it: Every arrow that flies feels the attraction of earth.

HENRY WADSWORTH LONGFELLOW

• Every man is worth just so much as the things are worth about which he busies himself.

MARCUS AURELIUS

• The general tendency of things throughout the world is to render mediocrity the ascendant power among mankind.

JOHN STUART MILL

• I hope to be remembered as someone who made the earth a little more beautiful.

WILLIAM O. DOUGLAS, FORMER ASSOCIATE JUSTICE

• The world is made of people who never quite get into the first team and who just miss the prizes at the flower show.

J. BRONOWSKI

• I have nothing to offer but blood, toil, sweat, and tears.

WINSTON CHURCHILL

• It is the quality of our work which will please God and not the quantity.

MAHATMA GANDHI

• Where quality is the thing sought after, the thing of supreme quality is cheap, whatever the price one has to pay for it.

WILLIAM JAMES

• Aim at perfection in everything, though in most things it is unattainable. However, they who aim at it and persevere will come much nearer to it than those whose laziness and despondency make them give it up as unattainable.

LORD CHESTERFIELD

• There is hardly anything in the world that some man cannot make a little worse and sell a little cheaper.

JOHN RUSKIN

CORNL

Work

We curse it, we neglect it, and many of us long for the day when we no longer have to do it. But our labors define who we are and give us reason to get up in the morning, to look forward to the future.

• Opportunity is missed by most people because it is dressed in overalls . . . .
THOMAS EDISON

• We work to become, not to acquire.
ELBERT HUBBARD

• Do not tell me how hard you work. Tell me how much you get done.
JAMES J. LING

• If you have great talents, industry will prove them; if moderate abilities, industry will supply their deficiencies.
SIR JOSHUA REYNOLDS

• I'm against retiring. The thing that keeps a man alive is having something to do. Sitting in a rocker never appealed to me.
COLONEL HARLAN SANDERS

• A farm is a hunk of land on which, if you get up early enough mornings and work late enough nights, you'll make a fortune—if you strike oil on it.
"FIBBER" MCGEE

• Times have changed. Forty years ago, people worked 12 hours a day, and it was called economic slavery. Now, they work 14 hours a day, and it's called moonlighting.
ROBERT ORBEN

• Let us be grateful to Adam; he cut us out of the blessing of idleness and won for us the curse of labor.
MARK TWAIN

• No labor, however humble, is dishonoring.
THE TALMUD

• Hard work is often an accumulation of the easy things you didn't do when you should have.

UNKNOWN

• Nothing is really work unless you would rather be doing something else.

JAMES MATTHEW BARRIE

• He who considers his work beneath him will be above doing it well.

ALEXANDER CHASE

• Unless you are willing to drench yourself in your work beyond the capacity of the average man, you are just not cut out for positions at the top.

J.C. PENNEY

• Some do the sowing, others the reaping.

ITALIAN PROVERB

• No one ever got very far by working a 40-hour week. Most of the notable people I know are trying to manage a 40-hour day.

CHANNING POLLOCK

• When your work speaks for itself, don't interrupt.

HENRY J. KAISER

• The darkest hour in any man's life is when he sits down to plan how to get money without earning it.

HORACE GREELEY

• You know what happens in the beehive? They kill those drones.

WILLIAM POAGE

• The successful people are the ones who can think up things for the rest of the world to keep busy at.

DON MARQUIS

• A man's . . . job is his bondage, but it also gives him a fair share of his identity and keeps him from being a bystander in somebody else's world.

MELVIN MADDOCKS

• As a remedy against all ills— poverty, sickness, and melancholy— only one thing is absolutely necessary: a liking for work.

CHARLES BAUDELAIRE

• Busy souls have no time to be busybodies.

AUSTIN O'MALLEY

• Work is what you do so that sometime you won't have to do it anymore.

ALFRED POLGAR

• If a man will not work, he shall not eat.

II THESSALONIANS 3: 10

• There is no such thing as a non-working mother.

HESTER MUNDIS

• Work is not man's punishment. It is his reward and his strength, his glory and his pleasure.

GEORGE SAND

Loneliness

When asked what loneliness was to her, one woman replied, "Having something wonderful happen to me and not having anyone to share it with." The next time you ask someone how things are going, slow down and take time to listen to the reply.

• For if they fall, the one will lift up his fellow: but woe to him that is alone when he falleth; for he hath not another to help him up.
ECCLESIASTES 4: 10

• Is not absence death to those who love?
ALEXANDER POPE

• Love consists in this, that two solitudes protect and touch and greet each other.
RAINER MARIA RILKE

• Solitude: A good place to visit, but a poor place to stay.
JOSH BILLINGS

• Loneliness is the first thing which God's eye named not good.
JOHN MILTON

• We ought not to isolate ourselves, for we cannot remain in a state of isolation. Social intercourse makes us the more able to bear with ourselves and with others.
JOHANN WOLFGANG VON GOETHE

• It would do the world good if every man in it would compel himself occasionally to be absolutely alone. Most of the world's progress has come out of such loneliness.
BRUCE BARTON

• There is a pleasure in the pathless woods; there is a rapture on the lonely shore; there is society, where none intrudes, by the deep sea, and music in its roar.
LORD BYRON

• Until I truly loved, I was alone.
CAROLINE NORTON

• Loneliness is only an opportunity to cut adrift and find yourself.
ANNA SHANNON MONROE

• Half the pleasure of solitude comes from having with us some friend to whom we can say how sweet solitude is.
W.M.L. JAY

• Language has created the word "loneliness" to express the pain of being alone, and the word "solitude" to express the glory of being alone.

PAUL TILLICH

• Leadership is the other side of the coin of loneliness, and he who is a leader must always act alone. And, acting alone, accept everything alone.

FERDINAND EDRALIN MARCOS

• . . . there are many who had rather meet their bitterest enemy in the field than their own hearts in their closet.

CHARLES CALEB COLTON

• Solitude is as needful to the imagination as society is wholesome for the character.

JAMES RUSSELL LOWELL

• The lonely one offers his hand too quickly to whomever he encounters.

FRIEDRICH NIETZSCHE

• Sometimes, when one person is missing, the whole world seems depopulated

ALPHONSE DE LAMARTINE

• I live in that solitude which is painful in youth but delicious in the years of maturity.

ALBERT EINSTEIN

• The right to be let alone is the most comprehensive of rights and the right most valued in civilized man.

LOUIS D. BRANDEIS, FORMER ASSOCIATE JUSTICE

• Anything for a quiet life, as the man said when he took the situation at the lighthouse.

CHARLES DICKENS

• In Genesis, it says that it is not good for a man to be alone; but sometimes it is a great relief.

JOHN BARRYMORE

• People are lonely because they build walls instead of bridges.

JOSEPH FORT NEWTON

• Absence extinguishes small passions and increases great ones, as the wind will blow out a candle and blow in a fire.

FRANÇOIS, DUC DE ROCHEFOUCAULD

• One may have a blazing hearth in one's soul, and yet no one ever comes to sit by it.

VINCENT VAN GOGH

• Man's loneliness is but his fear of life.

EUGENE O'NEILL

Art

Although some people go to museums to see art, others simply look through their windows to the landscape beyond. No matter where you are, art is there.

• Nature I loved, and, next to Nature, Art.

W.S. LANDOR

• People don't learn to enjoy pictures because they seldom look at them; and they seldom look at pictures because they have never learnt to enjoy them.

RAYMOND MORTIMER

• The day is coming when a single carrot, freshly observed, will set off a revolution.

PAUL CÉZANNE

• Never put more than two waves in a picture; it's fussy.

WINSLOW HOMER

• I try to apply colors like words that shape poems, like notes that shape music.

JOAN MIRÓ

• Have nothing in your houses that you do not know to be useful or believe to be beautiful.

WILLIAM MORRIS

• I paint from the top down. First the sky, then the mountains, then the hills, then the houses, then the cattle, and then the people.

GRANDMA MOSES

• A man of 80 has outlived probably three new schools of painting, two of architecture and poetry, and a hundred in dress.

JOYCE CAREY

• Art produces ugly things which frequently become beautiful with time.

JEAN COCTEAU

• An artist never really finishes his work, he merely abandons it.

PAUL VALÉRY

• Things are beautiful if you love them.

JEAN ANOUILH

• Sunshine can burn you, food can poison you, words can condemn you, pictures can insult you; music cannot punish—only bless.

ARTUR SCHNABEL

• I may not understand, but I am willing to admire.

ANTHONY HOPE

• Colors speak all languages.

JOSEPH ADDISON

• Life is a great big canvas, and you should throw all the paint on it you can.

DANNY KAYE

• All men are creative but few are artists.

PAUL GOODMAN

• I don't think of all the misery but of the beauty that still remains.

ANNE FRANK

• I adore art . . . when I am alone with my notes, my heart pounds and the tears stream from my eyes, and my emotion and my joys are too much to bear.

GIUSEPPE VERDI

• I write [music] as a sow piddles.

WOLFGANG AMADEUS MOZART

• It does not matter how badly you paint so long as you don't paint badly like other people.

GEORGE MOORE

• Without art, the crudeness of reality would make the world unbearable.

GEORGE BERNARD SHAW

• All the really good ideas I ever had came to me while I was milking a cow.

GRANT WOOD

• Every time an artist dies, part of the vision of mankind passes with him.

FRANKLIN DELANO ROOSEVELT

• How vain painting is—we admire the realistic depiction of objects which in their original state we don't admire at all.

BLAISE PASCAL

• Build your art horse-high, pig-tight, and bull-strong.

ELBERT HUBBARD

• A great artist can paint a great picture on a small canvas.

C.D. WARNER

• Art washes away from the soul the dust of everyday life.

PABLO PICASSO

CORNL

Morality

Take 12 people and ask them to define what is moral and what isn't and you'll get a dozen different answers. But here's something to think about. Your actions and words are your responsibility, and if you use those actions or words to knowingly hurt or offend someone, you have failed.

• Fault finding is a lot like window washing. All the dirt seems to be on the other side.

WALT REYNOLDS

• Character is what God and the angels know of us; reputation is what men and women think of us.

HORACE MANN

• The so-called new morality is too often the old immorality condoned.

LORD SHAWCROSS

• In great matters, men show themselves as they wish to be seen; in small matters, as they are.

GAMALIEL BRADFORD

• What is moral is what you feel good after.

ERNEST HEMINGWAY

• You are not very good if you are not better than your best friends imagine you to be.

JOHN CASPAR LAVATER

• Always do right. This will surprise some people and astonish the rest.

MARK TWAIN

• Be not merely good; be good for something.

HENRY DAVID THOREAU

• When a man sells 11 ounces for 12, he makes a compact with the devil, and sells himself for the value of an ounce.

HENRY WARD BEECHER

• I never knew an auctioneer to lie, unless it was absolutely necessary.

JOSH BILLINGS

• The right to do something does not mean that doing it is right.

WILLIAM SAFIRE

• No man can produce great things who is not thoroughly sincere in dealing with himself.

JAMES RUSSELL LOWELL

• The measure of a man is what he does with power.

PITTACUS

• Behavior is a mirror in which everyone displays his image.

JOHANN WOLFGANG VON GOETHE

• A righteous man hates false-hood, but a wicked man acts shamefully and disgracefully.

PROVERBS 13: 5

• It is not enough that you form, and even follow, the most excellent rules for conducting yourself in the world; you must also know when to deviate from them, and where lies the exception.

LORD GREVILLE

• In matters of conscience, the law of majority has no place.

MAHATMA GANDHI

• Nothing really immoral is ever permanently popular.

EDWARD GEORGE BULWER-LYTTON

• Make yourself an honest man, and then you may be sure that there is one rascal less in the world.

THOMAS CARLYLE

• All grand thoughts come from the heart.

MARQUIS DE VAUVENARGUES

• No man has a right to do as he pleases, except when he pleases to do right.

CHARLES SIMMONS

• A good man is kinder to his enemy than bad men to their friends.

BISHOP JOSEPH HALL

• The truth is, hardly any of us have ethical energy enough for more than one really inflexible point of honor.

GEORGE BERNARD SHAW

• In matters of prudence, last thoughts are best; in matters of morality, first thoughts.

ROBERT HALL

• It makes a great difference whether a person is unwilling to sin or does not know how.

SENECA

• Learn what a people glory in, and you may learn much of both the theory and practice of their morals.

JAMES MARTINEAU

• We rarely like the virtues we have not.

WILLIAM SHAKESPEARE

• There are two perfectly good men; one dead, and the other unborn.

CHINESE PROVERB

Technology

People often reminisce about the good ol' days. This doesn't mean they want to go back to mule teams and scrub boards, but they do yearn for a slower pace.

• Just the other day, I listened to a young fellow sing a very passionate song about how technology is killing us and all that. But before he started, he bent down and plugged his electric guitar into the wall socket.

PAUL GOODMAN

• Any sufficiently advanced technology is indistinguishable from magic.

ARTHUR C. CLARKE

• Art is I; science is we.

CLAUDE BERNARD

• If I have been able to see farther than others, it was because I stood on the shoulders of giants.

SIR ISAAC NEWTON

• But thou, O Daniel, shut up the words and seal the book, even to the time of the end; many shall run to and fro, and knowledge shall be increased.

DANIEL 12: 4

• Electronic calculators can solve problems which the man who made them cannot solve; but no Government-subsidized commission of engineers and physicists could create a worm.

JOSEPH WOOD KRUTCH

• The universe is full of magical things patiently waiting for our wits to grow sharper.

EDEN PHILLPOTS

• A world of science and great machines is still a world of men.

DAVID E. LILIENTHAL

• For tribal man, space was the uncontrollable mystery. For technological man, it is time that occupies the same role.

MARSHALL MCLUHAN

• God has no intention of setting a limit to the efforts of man to conquer space.

PIUS XII

• People are so overwhelmed with the prestige of their instruments that they consider their personal judgment of hardly any account.

PERCY WYNDHAM LEWIS

• Horsepower was a wonderful thing when only horses had it.

UNKNOWN

• Swept along in the concepts of their business-oriented culture, many people berate themselves if they are not as consistent and productive as machines.

GAY GAER LUCE

• It was naive of the 19th century optimists to expect paradise from technology—and it is equally naive of the 20th century pessimists to make technology the scapegoat for such old shortcomings as man's blindness, cruelty, immaturity, greed, and sinful pride.

PETER F. DRUCKER

• There are three ways of courting ruin: women, gambling, and calling in technicians.

GEORGES POMPIDOU

• If people really liked to work, we'd still be plowing the ground with sticks and transporting goods on our backs.

WILLIAM FEATHER

• In the space age, man will be able to go around the world in two hours—one hour for flying and the other to get to the airport.

NEIL MCELROY

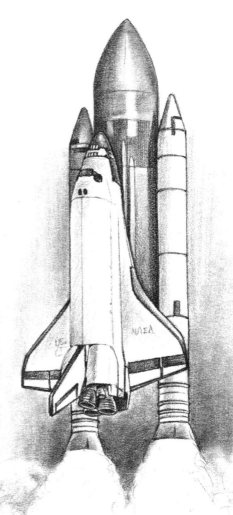

Silence

A brief silence before thunderous applause, a quiet moment for one who's gone. Silence often says more than any words could— and often says it better.

• Noise proves nothing. Often a hen who has merely laid an egg cackles as if she had laid an asteroid.
MARK TWAIN

• Secret and self-contained and solitary as an oyster.
CHARLES DICKENS

• You, having a large and fruitful mind, should not so much labor what to speak as to find what to leave unspoken. Rich soils are often to be weeded.
FRANCIS BACON

• Articulate words are a harsh clamor and dissonance. When man arrives at his highest perfection, he will again be dumb!
NATHANIEL HAWTHORNE

• You lose it if you talk about it.
ERNEST HEMINGWAY

• Man dwells apart, though not alone, / He walks among his peers unread; / The best of thoughts which he hath known/ For lack of listeners are not said.
JEAN INGELOW

• Silence composes the nerves.
CHARLOTTE BRONTÉ

• I'm exhausted from not talking.
SAMUEL GOLDWYN

• The next time you find yourself shouting at the top of your lungs, remember this: The noisy thunder does nothing; the silent lightning strikes.
UNKNOWN

• The habit of common and continuous speech is a symptom of mental deficiency.
WALTER BAGEHOT

• O golden Silence, bid our soul be still,/And on the foolish fretting of our care/ Lay thy soft touch of healing unaware!
JULIA DORR

• When you have spoken the word, it reigns over you. When it is unspoken, you reign over it.
ARABIAN PROVERB

• Next to entertaining or impressive talk, a thoroughgoing silence manages to intrigue most people.
FLORENCE HURST HARRIMAN

• There are moments when silence, prolong'd and unbroken, More expressive may be than all words ever spoken.
OWEN MEREDITH

• Shy and unready men are great betrayers of secrets; for there are few wants more urgent for the moment than the want of something to say.
HENRY TAYLOR

• It ain't a bad plan to keep still occasionally, even when you know what you're talking about.
KIN HUBBARD

• Be thou not rash with thy mouth . . . let thy words be few.
ECCLESIASTES 1: 2

• The flowering moments of the mind/ Drop half their petals in our speech.
OLIVER WENDELL HOLMES

• Listening is a magnetic and strange thing, a creative force. The friends who listen to us are the ones we move toward; we want to sit in their radius. When we are listened to, it creates us, makes us unfold and expand.
KARL MENNINGER

• Go placidly amid the noise and the haste, and remember what peace there may be in silence.
MAX EHRMANN

• In cities, no one is quiet but many are lonely; in the country, people are quiet but few are lonely.
GEOFFREY FRANCIS FISHER

• Men fear silence as they fear solitude because both give them a glimpse of the terror of life's nothingness.
ANDRÉ MAUROIS

• A ceremony of self-wastage— good talkers are miserable, they know that they have betrayed themselves, that they have taken material which should have a life of its own, to disperse it in noises upon the air.
CYRIL CONNOLLY

• In Maine, we have a saying that there's no point in speaking unless you can improve on silence.
EDMUND MUSKIE

• Quiet—that blessed mood.
WILLIAM WORDSWORTH

Tolerance

Intolerance knows no shades of gray. In its black-and-white world, argument replaces enlightenment. But tolerance allows differences of thought. It lets us color our culture with fairness.

• If we cannot end our differences, at least we can help make the world safe for diversity.

JOHN FITZGERALD KENNEDY

• Toleration . . . is the greatest gift of the mind; it requires the same effort of the brain that it takes to balance oneself on a bicycle.

HELEN KELLER

• Whoever kindles the flames of intolerance in America is lighting a fire underneath his own home.

HAROLD E. STASSEN

• We are all tolerant enough of those who do not agree with us, provided only they are sufficiently miserable.

DAVID GRAYSON

• People tolerate those they fear further than those they love.

EDGAR WATSON HOWE

• It is a good thing to demand liberty for ourselves and for those who agree with us, but it is a better thing and a rarer thing to give liberty to others who do not agree with us.

FRANKLIN DELANO ROOSEVELT

• Most people would rather defend to the death your right to say it than listen to it.

ROBERT BRAULT

• Broadmindedness is the result of flattening highmindedness out.

GEORGE SAINTSBURY

• Let your precept be, "Be easy."

RICHARD STEELE

• There is a limit at which forbearance ceases to be a virtue.

EDMUND BURKE

• I hate people who are intolerant.

LAURENCE J. PETER

• No man has a right in America to treat any other man tolerantly, for tolerance is the assumption of superiority.

WENDELL WILLKIE

• Broadminded is just another way of saying a fellow's too lazy to form an opinion.

WILL ROGERS

• It is easy to be tolerant of the principles of other people if you have none of your own.

HERBERT SAMUEL

• People are very openminded about new things—as long as they're exactly like the old ones.

CHARLES F. KETTERING

• Tolerance comes with age. I see no fault committed that I myself could not have committed at some time or other.

JOHANN WOLFGANG VON GOETHE

• I have seen gross intolerance shown in support of tolerance.

SAMUEL TAYLOR COLERIDGE

• If you will please people, you must please them in their own way; and as you cannot make them what they should be, you must take them as they are.

LORD CHESTERFIELD

• When my friends are one-eyed, I try to see them in profile.

JOSEPH JOUBERT

• The trouble with being tolerant is that people think you don't understand the problem.

MERLE L. MEACHAM

• We hand folks over to God's mercy and show none ourselves.

GEORGE ELIOT

• He maketh his sun to rise on the evil and on the good, and sendeth rain on the just and on the unjust.

MATTHEW 5: 45

Generosity

One of the greatest by-products of a generous act is that it inspires more generous acts.

• We are all here on Earth to help others; what on Earth the others are here for, I don't know.
W.H. AUDEN

• If a friend is in trouble, don't annoy him by asking if there is anything you can do. Think up something appropriate, and do it.
EDGAR WATSON HOWE

• There are eight rungs in charity. The highest is when you help a man to help himself.
MAIMONIDES

• Those who give hoping to be rewarded with honor are not giving; they are bargaining.
PHILO

• I have tried to teach people that there are three kicks in every dollar: one, when you make it—and how I love to make a dollar; two, when you have it—and I have the Yankee lust for saving. The third kick is when you give it away—and it is the biggest kick of all.
WILLIAM ALLEN WHITE

• Nowadays, we think of a philanthropist as someone who donates big sums of money; yet the word is derived from two Greek words, philos (loving) and anthropos (man), loving man. All of us are capable of being philanthropists. We can give of ourselves.
EDWARD LINDSAY

• If you haven't got any charity in your heart, you have the worst kind of heart trouble.
BOB HOPE

• If you're in trouble, or hurt or need—go to the poor people. They're the only ones that'll help—the only ones.
JOHN STEINBECK

• Doing good is the only certainly happy action of a man's life.

SIR PHILIP SIDNEY

• Be charitable before wealth makes thee covetous.

SIR THOMAS BROWNE

• In this world it is not what we take up, but what we give up, that makes us rich.

HENRY WARD BEECHER

• Be charitable and indulgent to every one but thyself.

JOSEPH JOUBERT

• What I gave, I have; what I spent, I had; what I kept, I lost.

OLD EPITAPH

• He who gives what he would as readily throw away, gives without generosity; for the essence of generosity is in self-sacrifice.

SIR HENRY TAYLOR

• Give, and it shall be given unto you; good measure, pressed down and shaken together, and running over.

LUKE 6: 38

• A man is sometimes more generous when he has but a little money than when he has plenty, perhaps through fear of being thought to have but little.

BENJAMIN FRANKLIN

• Almost always the most indigent are the most generous.

STANISLAW I OF POLAND

• A bone to the dog is not charity. Charity is the bone shared with the dog, when you are just as hungry as the dog.

HENRY HOME

• The best portion of a good man's life; his little, nameless, unremembered acts of kindness and love.

WILLIAM WORDSWORTH

Imagination

The words "pretend like" begin every little child's game. The children are princesses one day, castaways the next, soldiers and cowboys and pirates or movie stars. For them, anything is possible. The children become adults, but they don't have to leave their imaginations behind.

• Personally, I would sooner have written *Alice in Wonderland* than the whole *Encyclopaedia Britannica*.

STEPHEN LEACOCK

• I played with an idea and grew wilful; tossed it into the air and transformed it; let it escape and recaptured it; made it iridescent with fancy, and winged it with paradox.

OSCAR WILDE

• Imagination is more important than knowledge.

ALBERT EINSTEIN

• I have learned this at least by my experiment: that if one advances confidently in the direction of his dreams, and endeavors to live the life which he has imagined, he will meet with a success unexpected in common hours.

HENRY DAVID THOREAU

• Anyone who limits his vision to his memories of yesterday is already dead.

NOEL B. GERSON

• Sleep leads to dreaming / waking to imagination and to/ imagine what we/could be, O, / what we could be.

SUSAN GRIFFIN

• I used to lie awake as a child and get more entertainment and terror out of blank walls and plain furniture than most children could find in a toy store.

CHARLOTTE PERKINS GILMAN

• So long as we have faith in our fairy tales, we are none the worse.

ELLEN GLASGOW

• The trouble with the average human being is that he never goes on mountain journeys. He stops at the first way station and refuses to believe there is a country beyond.

AGNES SLIGH TURNBULL

• Better a dish of illusion and a hearty appetite for life than a feast of reality and indigestion therewith.

HARRY A. OVERSTREET

• No matter how old you get, if you can keep the desire to be creative, you're keeping the man-child alive.

JOHN CASSAVETES

• Mozart is the human incarnation of the divine force of creation.

JOHANN WOLFGANG VON GOETHE

• When I am completely myself, entirely alone, or during the night when I cannot sleep, it is on such occasions that my ideas flow best and most abundantly. Whence and how these come I know not, nor can I force them. Nor do I hear in my imagination the parts successively, but I hear them *gleich alles zusammen* (at the same time all together).

WOLFGANG AMADEUS MOZART

• And the Lord God formed man of the dust of the ground, and breathed into his nostrils the breath of life; and the man became a living soul.

GENESIS 2: 7

• Words: The hummingbirds of the imagination.

ELBERT HUBBARD

• Imagination grows by exercise, and contrary to common belief, is more powerful in the mature than in the young.

W. SOMERSET MAUGHAM

• Isn't it splendid to think of all the things there are to find out about? It just makes me feel glad to be alive—it's such an interesting world. It wouldn't be half so interesting if we knew all about everything, would it? There'd be no scope for imagination then, would there?

LUCY MONTGOMERY
(FROM *ANNE OF GREEN GABLES*)

Planning

Without a charted course, the ship never sails from the harbor. Without a game strategy, the football team never leaves the bench. Without a blueprint, the building can never be constructed. Not a whole lot that's right happens sheerly by accident.

• He who every morning plans the transactions of the day, and follows out that plan, carries a thread that will guide him through the labyrinth of the most busy life. But where no plan is laid, where the disposal of time is surrendered merely to the chance of incidence, chaos will soon reign.

VICTOR HUGO

• Everyone has a will to win, but very few have a will to prepare to win.

VINCE LOMBARDI

• A sense of the value of time— that is, of the best way to divide one's time into one's various activities—is an essential preliminary to efficient work; it's the only method of avoiding hurry.

ARNOLD BENNETT

• You will never "find" time for anything. If you want time, you must make it.

CHARLES BUXTON

• When a man does not know what harbor he is making for, no wind is the right wind.

SENECA

• The more human beings proceed by plan, the more efficiently they may be hit by accident.

FRIEDRICH DURRENMATT

• We must ask where we are and whither we are tending.

ABRAHAM LINCOLN

• Nothing is more terrible than activity without insight.

THOMAS CARLYLE

• Don't agonize. Organize.

FLORENCE R. KENNEDY

• Have a time and place for everything and do everything in its time and place, and you will not only accomplish more, but have far more leisure than those who are always hurrying, as if vainly attempting to overtake time that had been lost.

TYRON EDWARDS

• Adventure is the result of poor planning.

COLONEL BLATCHFORD SNELL

• Long-range planning does not deal with future decisions but with the future of present decisions.

PETER DRUCKER

• Things almost always turn out otherwise than one anticipates.

MAURICE HULST

• You can never plan the future by the past.

EDMUND BURKE

• To have his path made clear for him is the aspiration of every human being in our beclouded and tempestuous existence.

JOSEPH CONRAD

• I must create a system or be enslaved by another man's.

WILLIAM BLAKE

• My life has no purpose, no direction, no aim, no meaning, and yet I'm happy. I can't figure it out. What am I doing right?

CHARLES M. SCHULTZ

• The men who succeed are the efficient few. They are the few who have the ambition and willpower to develop themselves.

HERBERT N. CASSON

• What can a man do who doesn't know what to?

MILTON MAYER

• Life is what happens to us while we are making other plans.

THOMAS LA MANCE

Pencil Art by Ray E. Watkins, Jr.
Design by Bob Nance.
Cover Photo by Vann Cleveland.
Printing and binding by Thomson-Shore, Inc.